CW01020890

Tractor Ted
TED 1
Showtime

TOM YEOMAN
Spearhead
1st
TED 1
It's Showtime and the tractor is getting the showring ready.

**The animals have started to arrive.
Everybody is excited.**

The animals are washed. They have to look their best for the show.

Their legs are cleaned,

their tails are cleaned and...

even their horns are cleaned.

1st
TED 1
This cow's coat is being dried so it looks all fluffy.

Once they are ready they are given a lovely straw bed to lie on.

Soon the shed is full with cattle all waiting for the show to start.

Outside people are getting their stands ready.

ATTWOOLLS
S100
1st
TED 1
This stand has tractors
and quad bikes for sale.

This stand is selling delicious cheese.

1st
TED 1
The sheep are being groomed ready for the show.

The children love to help.

1st
TED 1
This sheep has a cosy rug to keep him warm and clean.

There are so many different sheep here....

spotty ones...

woolly ones,

ones with curly horns, and ones with fluffy hair.

At the show there is so much to see. There are old fashioned tractors

steam engines

LADYBIRD
1st
TED 1
and sometimes even
train rides to go on.

It's showtime and this man is a judge. It is his job to choose the winner.

He is looking for the best pig.

This pig has won first prize – well done!

McCORMICK
1st
TED 1
The tractors are hard at work.

They are moving the fences for the horses to jump over.

The horses must jump very high.

Now it is time for the children to show their calves.

Some are very well behaved.
1st
TED 1

Some are very naughty.

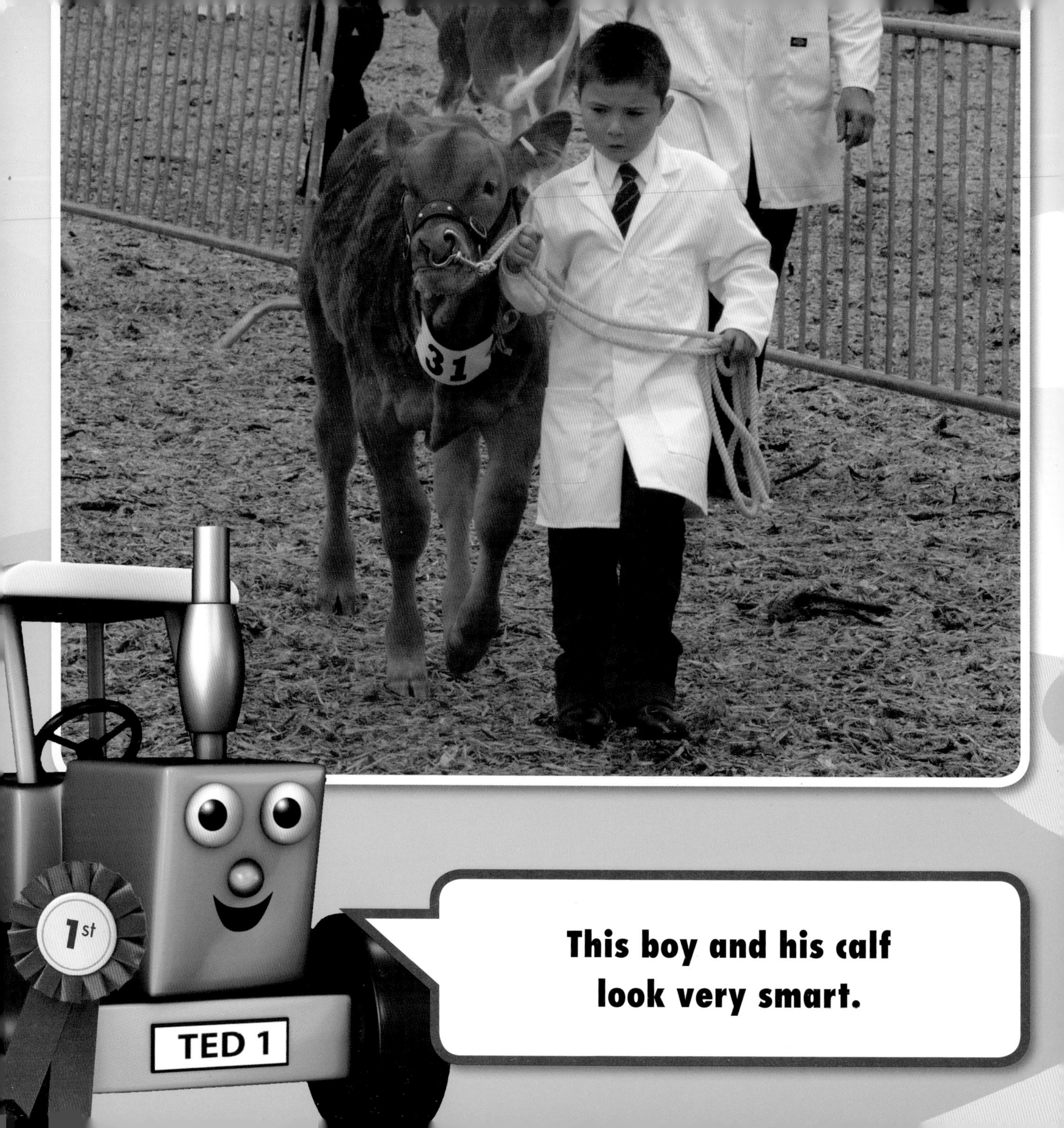

This boy and his calf look very smart.

Well done, they won first prize.

Which animal would you like to show?

What part of the cow is being washed?

The leg

The tail

The horns

1st

TED 1

How many sheep are in the show ring?